Leading Without Dollars

Vol. I - Basic Leadership Principles

by Eric K. Dargan

Newly Revised

Copyright © 2023 Eric K. Dargan

All rights reserved. No part of this publication may be reproduced, stored in a retrieval system or transmitted in any form or by any means, electronic, mechanical, photocopying, recording or otherwise without permission of the copyright owner.

To request permissions, contact the publisher at ssermas@typingmonekpublishers.com

ISBN 979-8-9876600-1-0

All images by Diane Binnie Photography. All rights reserved.
Cover Design by Kimberly Platt.

Published by Typing Monkey Publishers, LLC
www.typingmonkeypublishers.com

Acknowledgments

To all the people that have touched and impacted my life in so many ways, I say a big thank you!

There are some people that I must specifically thank. Thank you to my late father, Booker T. W. Dargan, for raising me to be a man of my word and showing me how to take care of a family. I thank my mother, Annie Ruth Dargan, for showing me compassion and how to love all people. I thank First Missionary Baptist Church of Blytheville, AR, for being instrumental in my growth as a child and in Christ as well as showing me how to serve my fellow man. I thank Prairie View A&M University and Michigan State University for lifelong friendships and preparing me for my professional life. I thank all the employees at Southwestern Bell Telephone/SBC (now AT&T) that contributed to my growth and development in becoming a professional leader. I thank the City of Houston for allowing me to serve at one of the highest levels in Public Works as well as the City of San Diego for allowing me to serve as their Chief Operating Officer. I thank Diane Lowery-Binnie for encouraging and pushing me to write this book. Diane is also the photographer who provided all the breath-taking photos. I thank Debra Pruitt who has been my Executive Assistant and editor for the last 21 years. I thank my late wife of 24 years, Tracy Arnese Dargan, for our life journey and two intelligent and beautiful children, Eric II and Traci Symone. I thank my wife, Iris Savage Dargan, for her love and support in editing and encouraging me to republish Volume 1. Lastly, I thank you for supporting me.

TABLE OF CONTENTS

Foreword	2
Introduction	4
Know Thyself	6
Bees Can't Fly	9
First Impressions	11
Communication	12
F.E.A.R.	15
What is Your Passion?	16
Applied Knowledge is Power	18
Everyone Deserves Respect	21
Remove "NO" from Your Vocabulary	22
Feedback	25
Put Your People on a Pedestal	26
Birds of a Feather, Flock Together	28
Build a Talented and Likable Team	30
No Man is an Island	33
You Cannot Please Everyone	34
Dream	37
Conclusion	39

Foreword

I have known Eric K. Dargan for many years; both professionally and through some very trying times in our personal lives where we've supported each other and have gotten through. He's an honorable man who expects only the best out of others. For him to write such an inspiring book as *Leading Without Dollars* is proof of his integrity and character.

Words simply cannot describe the sincerity and reasoning behind this brilliantly written step-by-step coaching for business success. If you want success in your business, here's how to obtain it!

This book is well thought out, timelessly written, and executed! Whether you utilize it in your business career today, beginning stages or advanced. At any level of education, from high school to college graduate, it's a great addition for success; your success and this book not only goes hand in hand, and it can also be a great gift!

I'm truly honored to have read this book; but more importantly, to apply these very principles and best practices in my own business career. You're never too young or old when it comes to business to better your career and/or just being at your best.

We all can reference this book and apply it into practice. Then see the difference in how we perform in the paths we've chosen for ourselves.

Ask yourself...
1. Can I see myself advancing to my next level?
2. Am I ready for the next level?
3. Do I want to be successful in my career?

Well reader, if you answered "Yes" it is time for you to get to the next level in your business career. This book will help you in your efforts in becoming the best you can be in your business. I'm excited about this book and looking forward to what's next from the heart, mind, and thoughts of Author Eric K. Dargan, who sincerely wants what's best for you. This book will help you get to where you want to be by using these precise principles for your success in business and in life. "It is simply not enough to be the best when you have the ability to be GREAT!" Be encouraged....

 Bestselling Author Donald Williams
 In Times of Need, Poems of Encouragement

Introduction

Thirty-two years ago, I started my professional career. I graduated with a BS in Electrical Engineering from Prairie View A&M University followed by a MS in Electrical Engineering from Michigan State University.

Thinking I would be a computer design engineer, my life turned in another direction when I was offered the opportunity to pursue a management track versus being technical. I have spent the last thirty-two years of my career in management, and I have never looked back. Within my first year, I realized that anyone could be a manager, but it took a different type of person to be a leader.

That's where this journey begins. How do you stand out among thirty-five new managers all destined to be CEOs of a major corporation? Leaders really are developed, not born; and that development is not accomplished in a short period of time. It starts early in life and exposure to as many types of people as possible plays into it. It doesn't matter if you work in corporate America, the military, the private sector, or the public sector, leading without dollars takes a special skill.

Often in public and nonprofit organizations we are faced with financial woes and shortages. When revenues fall short or expenses exceed the budget, the first things cut are travel and training. It's difficult to develop employees when there is no funding. The leadership principles in this book are the basic characteristics of a sound leader regardless of funding and much needed resources.

Eric K. Dargan

Know Thyself

Be confident in who you are. Know your capabilities and capacity. Don't bend when the wind blows. Exhibit strength and confidence in all circumstances; especially, during trials and tribulations. Be humble in your dealings with others. Don't be someone you are not. Remember that confidence is arrogance under control.

Be able to "walk with kings; nor lose the common touch."
-Rudyard Kipling, "If"

Bees Can't Fly

Theoretically, the wing span of the bumble bee is not wide enough to lift the body weight of the bee. Therefore, aerodynamically the bee should not be able to fly.

Since the bee never went to college to learn aerodynamics nor did any of the more mature and wiser bees tell him he couldn't fly, the bee defies nature and achieves the success of flight because he believes he can.

If you bee-lieve, you can achieve!

First Impressions

It really is true that you don't get a second chance to make a first impression. It does not matter if you are a lawn maintenance worker or the CEO of a major corporation, how you present yourself will influence how others respond to you.

It is what you wear and how you wear it that creates the first impression. Whether you are in a uniform or in a suit, presentation matters.

Looking good can also make you feel good about yourself.

It's your choice to create what you want others to see in you.

Communication

Communication is best when more senses are used. Because you can use sight, sound, and touch, face-to-face interaction is considered one of the most effective modes of communication. By seeing a person's body language, hearing their tone, and shaking their hand, gives the receiver context of what the person communicating is actually saying.

When we communicate in ways other than face-to-face, we lose access to some of our senses. For example, with videoconferencing, we can only see and hear; with phone calls, we can only hear, and with email or text, we can only see. Limiting your senses can allow things to be lost in translation.

All modes of communication serve a purpose. As leaders we must be intentional about which mode we use to communicate most effectively.

Communicate with as many senses as possible.

F.E.A.R.
False Evidence Appearing Real

Don't buy into stereotypes and don't believe everything you read in the papers or see on television. Society sells products and creates delusions through fear. Whether it's police brutality, neighborhood crime, insurance or hand sanitizer, fear is normally the driving factor. Do your own research and form your own opinion/position based on facts versus hearsay on a particular subject. Remember the old saying, "Believe half of what you see and none of what you hear!"

Control your thoughts and actions with positive influences that have substance and proof.

What is Your Passion?

- What do you dream about regularly?
- What job would you gladly perform for free?
- What makes you smile?
- What makes your heart beat rapidly?
- What takes your breath away?

Answer these questions and then develop your plan to achieve your passion. Don't put it off.

Tomorrow is not promised.
Yesterday is the past.
Today is the present.

Savor the gift of life.

Applied Knowledge is Power

The saying 'Knowledge is Power' is often credited to Sir Francis Bacon; however, traces of this saying actually can be found in the early 600's by Imam Ali. Knowledge is wonderful to possess, but when it's not applied, it's useless. There are so many intelligent people in the world that do not see the gift they were given. When talent and brilliance is not used, it's lost. Whether a person is born with greatness or develops skill and knowledge over time, if they apply it daily, their contributions to society will be immeasurable.

Power is gained by sharing knowledge, not hoarding it.

Everyone Deserves Respect

Do unto others **better** than you would have them do unto you.

Everyone wants to be loved, appreciated, and respected. To be loved one should give love. To be appreciated one should show appreciation. To be respected one must give respect. At work and in life, the way we treat and respect those in authority, should also be the way we treat and respect those who are not. For example, the way you would treat the Mayor should be the same way you would treat the custodian.

We reap what we sow. That is why oftentimes, the energy we receive from others is equivalent to the energy we give out.

If we are the light that shines on the mountaintop, others will be the light to guide us through the darkness of the valley.

Respecting others shows character.

Remove "NO" from Your Vocabulary

No one likes to be told "No." Even if the answer is "No," there's always a reason why. Try answering all questions with "Yes," and explain what has to happen to attain that answer. "No" basically means you either lack the resources or the desire. Resources can be easily explained and maybe with the proper "Ask," can be attained. Be open minded and don't allow a negative mindset to keep you or others from moving forward.

Never EVER Give Up!

Feedback

It's What You Say AND How You Say It

Feedback can be received positively or negatively based on the choice of words and the tone used. As leaders, your words carry weight and the way it lands on your audience of one or many depends a lot on your delivery. Understanding your audience and the sensitivity of the subject should always be considered when addressing a crowd or an individual.

Be positive, truthful, transparent, compassionate, collaborative, and direct. How you say things is important, however, don't lose the meat of the message by sugar coating either.

A great leader can terminate an employee, give them a hug, and remain friends for a lifetime.

Say what you mean, mean what you say, but don't be mean when you say it!

Put Your People on a Pedestal

In any organization, the greatest resource is the people that work for you. As it is often said in business, "doing more with less" or "doing more with no more" is everyday life. As leaders, human capital is the greatest investment that we have in our possession. How we treat that investment, how we grow that investment, and how we appreciate that investment determines the size of the dividends we receive.

Your best long-term investment is your human capital.

Birds of a Feather,

Be mindful of those you hang around. Do they value life the way you do? Do they strive to achieve better? Do they believe a higher power is directing them?

Flock Together

People with whom we interact daily influence our thoughts and actions. Your circle of influence should be either where you want to be or together everyone should be moving in the same direction.

You attract who you are!

Build a Talented
and

It goes unsaid that a team with talent will achieve success. But, can talent alone sustain their success? Likable people make attaining the goal fun. Likable people create a positive work environment which leads to productivity and retention.

Likable Team

Likable people are given the benefit of the doubt and are shown mercy in difficult situations.

Talent is good, but it is even better when others want you on their team.

No Man is an Island

Successful people do not reach success by themselves. Often there are mentors that have assisted in laying a foundation or guiding them through the maze of life. As you climb the ladder of success, reach back and pull someone along with you.

As you help others, you will find that others will be there to help you.

You Cannot Please Everyone . . .

There was a man sitting down for supper with his twelve closest friends. A woman washed his feet and then rubbed his feet with expensive oil. Some of his friends chastised him for allowing her to waste oil that could have been sold and profits given to the poor. But they did not see the vision. She was preparing his body for burial. There will always be others who don't like the direction or decisions you make.

Everybody may not see your vision.

Dream

Close your eyes...

Allow your mind to drift towards your most intimate desires. Imagine the location you wish to live. Picture the house where you find peace and solitude. Who is laying beside you with their arms wrapped around you? Imagine that place of work that causes you to leap out of bed every morning. Now wake up and turn your dreams into reality.

Only you control your destiny.

Conclusion

I pray that this book has touched you in some way. Leadership is not a complicated science. It's really a behavior. It's how we communicate and respond to life issues on a daily basis. The successes achieved and failures faced are the results of choices we make every day. The one factor that we have complete control over is "Ourselves." We control the choices and decisions we make; we do not control others and how they respond.

We can choose to live free. We can choose to serve others. We can choose to love hard. We can choose to do the very best we can in every situation. I believe at the end of the day; great leaders choose to make God happy with every decision they make.

www.ingramcontent.com/pod-product-compliance
Lightning Source LLC
LaVergne TN
LVRC090441090526
838199LV00117B/540